W9-CLQ-350

My Youth Like Petals

My Youth Like Petals

A Convent Memoir

ᔓ

Charlotte Barr

My Youth Like Petals: A Convent Memoir

by

Charlotte Barr

Copyright © 2016 by Charlotte Barr. All rights reserved.

Except for brief quotations in a review, this book, or any part thereof, may not be reproduced in any form without prior written permission from the publisher. For information, please address The Intermundia Press, LLC at www.theintermundiapress.com.

ISBN 978-1-887730-49-5

Printed in the United States of America.

Published by

)Ip(

THE INTERMUNDIA PRESS, LLC
a Delaware company

Front cover photograph courtesy of Cheryl Merin Barr.

Back cover photograph of Sister Mary Anthony Barr courtesy of Joe Horton Studio: Sister Mary Anthony's final graduation, Saint Cecilia Academy at Overbrook, May 1990.

I will scatter my youth like
Petals before Your Face

—Poor Clare Rite of Profession

This book that contains so much of the
life we shared is fondly dedicated to
My Sisters of the Dominican Diaspora

I love you, too, for being a survivor.
Except for once when caught to heaven and
Once thrown to earth, you sailed in fog.
From you I've learned to dwell as though departing,
And past all christologies to cling to Christ.

—Sister Mary Anthony Barr
"Letter to Paul," *Sister Woman*

And to my old shoe, Marida,
Sister Mary Angela Highfield, OP

Then I pray the harder that the hungry mouth of Lethe
Won't consume such crumbs as my remembrance
Scatters in the wood between our solitudes and am
Consoled that what one discards becomes the other's hand.
The wonder of love is nothing's lost but what is not bestowed.
Yes, your gifts enfold, enfoil, they harbor me.
I send you word that I am happy; life is rich; I sing.

—Sister Mary Anthony Barr
"Solitaire," *Sister Woman*

And lastly, everlastingly, to the memory of

Peter Joseph Heidenrich

Here we were, you and I, and between us Christ was a third.

Epigraph

I CHOSE THE TITLE OF this book from an ancient rite of religious consecration not only for its symbolic expression of self-giving, but also for its floral imagery. It recalled my friend Sister Mary Bernard's description of our youth in the consecrated life: "We were in our floruit." The literal meaning of the word designates the period in the past when a person was most active. But the etymology is what attracted me: "flowering." As young sisters, we were in the first bloom of enthusiasm and idealism. We were, as the beloved in the Song of Songs, "a garden enclosed," and our flowers were reserved for our Beloved.

As we grew older in religious life, our salad days seemed a distant memory, and the vibrant flowers of youth faded and drooped even to the undimmed eyes of faith. And so my friend and I found comfort in the words of our mutually admired poet, William Butler Yeats: "The spring vegetables may be over, but they are never refuted."

Contents

Publisher's Foreword

"ATTENTIVENESS," ACCORDING TO THE Oratorian priest, Nicholas Malebranche (1638–1715) via the cultural and literary critic, Walter Benjamin, "is the natural prayer of the soul." Charlotte Barr's *My Youth Like Petals: A Convent Memoir* is just such an attentive book. It is an honor and a privilege to have been asked to write a foreword that attends to the soul of this book.

Permit me a digression regarding memoir. At best, a memoir retains its French ancestry of being a dissertation. I'm not necessarily referring to a long disquisition that a student cobbles together toward a graduate degree; rather, I am thinking about dissertation's being derived from the Latin, *disserere*, to continue to discuss, to examine further. Thus the French *mémoire* has everything to do with discussing or examining further the recollection of something with regard to one's life.

It is unfortunate that many contemporary published memoirs have devolved into narcissistic popular exposés that are either forgotten not long after they've been published or become more mere tabloid fodder. Offhand, I can think of a few that enjoyed a number of weeks on the *New York Times* bestseller list and faded into obscurity soon thereafter, though one can ostensibly find copies at overstock booksellers.

It's not cruel to speak of such things. It's just that I am convinced that (1) the *New York Times* bestseller list is no indicator that a popular book is either well-written or a good read or—it just sells well, due mostly to the efforts of a well-oiled marketing machine; and (2) the books implicated are merely examples of unmemorable memoirs of the devolved sort whose renown was due to some previously experienced Andy Warholic 15 minutes of fame in other literary or celebrity endeavors. Not so with this convent memoir.

Why? I think it has to do with the act of encountering. As you read, you will not only engage with the encounters the author has with others within her life. The encounter is between the author, Charlotte Barr, and you, dear reader. The topos, in other words, the convent life and beyond of a religious, is also the encounter between you and Ms. Barr, initiating meetings with otherness in ways that expose us, make us vulnerable, even uncertain about our own identity. Jungian analyst John Hill has said that such deep encounters "revive memories of a lost wholeness and reconnect us with the mystery of our being and the world around us."[1] Returning to the poets, in a letter to his brother and sister-in-law, George and Georgina, John Keats put it this way: "Call the world, if you please, 'The vale of soul-making.'"[2] In fact, it's not just soul-making but soul-deepening you will experience within these pages.

The crazy epithet, *religious*, occurs within this book's pages, too, not as an adjective denoting piety (often to the point of pretentiousness and snobbish elitism) but rather *religious* as a noun. In my salad days, I pastored the Little Stone Church on picturesque Mackinac Island, Michigan. One morning, I had coffee with a couple who were longtime members of this resort community parish. Comfortably seated in a high-backed wicker chair on their front porch, Mrs. F. addressed me at point blank range, "Eric, are you a religious?" I wasn't sure that I'd heard her correctly, for I thought that I was in fact being asked if I was *a*religious, in other words, not influenced by or practicing religion. Silly me. Quickly, I recovered from my instantaneous reverie, realizing that in her perceptive way, my interlocutor asked if I was capable of maintaining the delicate balance between religion as *religare* and as *religere*.

If we look at the word *religious*, we find that bound up in its meaning is the notion of reflection and connection that implies freedom to examine, ponder, and reflect upon every sort of experience in a personal way. This comes from looking at "religious" as coming from *religere*. Looking at "religious" from another vantage point—that of *religare*—we note that included in this word is the meaning "to be tied or bound back to a previous state of existence." This derivation of *religious* usually means unflagging adherence to a creed, unwavering devotion to a particular dogma, belief, or set thereof.

As *religare*, such tying or binding back to a previous state of existence evokes images of Prometheus fettered to the craggy hillside in punishment for having brought fire to human beings without divine authority. *Religere* calls to mind the image of the sojourning spiritual pilgrim "caught" between the reality of this world and the next; he or she is depicted as entering a new dimension, allowing us to fully realize our own set-apartness in our encounter not only with other individuals but ourselves as other. The alchemists of medieval and enlightenment times saw this in their symbolism of the wingéd and flightless birds, black and white, yin and yang, forever bound to one another in their eternal process of transformation—it's not a once-for-all-time event, after all. A religious, then, maintains the delicate balance between these two "polarities," these two "opposites"of binding and freedom to explore, sometimes favoring one or the other, occasionally favoring neither at all.

As difficult as this balancing act is, then, why not look at how one must let go of an old situation, old feelings, what one has become and grown accustomed to, the routines, the ruts in which one becomes mired, the perceptions and visions one has formed and has, even the memory of all that and the confabulations associated with such memories? Once we allow the silt to settle in our personal streams, we rediscover that such is the beginning of an awakening to the moment of un-forgetting: *anamnesis*. This is not phenomenologically the way remembering is, because in the act of anamnesis, of unforgetting, we become or already are the figure in itself that we recollect. It is the difference between having one's memories like limbs put back where they belong, as in the case of Dionysos, and commencing an erratic, chaotic effort to recall. As an example of anamnesis, we have only to look at the Eucharist, in which the bread, the body of the Christ, undergoes oblation (*oblatio*, offering to God); fraction, or breaking (*fractio*); and anamnesis, or recollection. That it is chaotic indicates a rootedness in origins, the primordial, the vale of the world wherein soul-making and soul-deepening take place.

Put aside the debates over transubstantiation and consubstantiation, for what is at stake is what in translations of the Greek New Testament as "Do this in remembrance of me," is more accurately rendered as, "Do this in anamnesis of—in an effort to recall—me (Τοῦτο ποιεῖτε εἰς τὴν ἐμὴν ἀνάμνησιν·)."

When we speak of anamnesis as "unforgetting" rather than as "re-membering," we enact an uncertainty. We attempt to build a bridge between ourselves and the origin of forgetting. Anamnesis at bottom is a search—hence re-call, re-collection—whereas remembering is re-membering, piecing back together, putting the fragments of *mnēmē* into a reasonable semblance or facsimile of how it was before the memory was lost or forgotten. Remembering is memory as prosthesis. Such memory—remembering—has at its core gimmickry, if not trickery, involved. For example, one creates mnemonic *devices* to associate objects with, say, the names of people. There are even hucksters willing to sell us kits with claims of developing better memory, guaranteed, and only costing three payments of $69.99 (plus shipping and handling, as well as state and local taxes)!

Anamnesis, however, is a search. It might be successful. It

might end in total failure. The search, regardless of the outcome, is what matters.

The writing that you encounter in these pages of *My Youth Like Petals* is of the sort that increases our sensitivity as readers. In bringing herself into this kind of writing, Charlotte Barr brings us to encounter ourselves by her very presence in this work. And this is anamnesis: embodied unforgetting enacted by the writer who from the very first sentence is in the world through more than compassionate involvement with it.

So soul, having clapped your hands and sung and louder sung, come up onto the porch. Pull up a chair. Welcome home and join in this feast that through our sharing, we will come to know, understand, and become better attuned to ourselves.

Eric Killinger

Memorial Day 2016
Santa Fe, New Mexico

My Youth Like Petals

Like Petals

A Convent Memoir

THERE WAS AS YET NO Peace Corps in 1960. For idealistic Catholic girls, there was the convent. We wanted to be the Little Flower. My confirmation name—chosen by my father, a devout convert—was Theresa. We wanted to be saints, to be married to Christ. I had spent my junior year abroad but other than that had no experience of the world. I turned eighteen less than a month before I entered the convent on September 3, 1960. One doesn't just join a religious community. It is always an entrance, as dramatic as any on the stage. And the entrance is more than a door; it is a portal, a threshold, a gateway between two worlds. Though technically one is an aspirant, a postulant, one who asks admittance, and the door swings open in both directions, allowing the newcomer to leave or be discharged at any time, this passage is a transforming step and whether one stays briefly or long an irrevocable one. More candidates leave religious life than stay, but the mark of the cloister is permanent. My mother was unhappy about this decision. I suppose she wanted grandchildren. Mostly, she knew how immature I was and that I wasn't ready for such a commitment. My father supported my decision, but he was losing his little girl.

Neither of my parents made that trip from Chattanooga to Nashville. My brother, Nelson, and my friend, John Collison, drove me to Saint Cecilia that bright autumn day. They were cohorts who shared my dream. Nelson would soon be Frater Reginald, a Dominican friar in Somerset, Ohio, and John Frater Paschal, a Benedictine monk at Saint Bernard Abbey in Cullman, Alabama. My brother left as a novice and went to New York to work for Dorothy Day at *The Catholic Worker*. He lived in Greenwich Village and became one of the "Beat Poets" of the '60s. Nelson hitchhiked to Bardstown, Kentucky, prior to my profession in 1962 to meet my Trappist hero, Father Louis—Thomas Merton—and sent me a holy card signed by Father Louis, who was then novice master at the Abbey of Gethsemani. A year earlier, John had sent me the crucifix for my fifteen-mystery rosary when I got the habit. He later went to New York, too, and disappeared from my life.

I stayed for thirty years. My other two high school and novitiate companions, Sister Mary Angela and Sister Luke, are still there. Of the eight of us who entered as postulants, they and Sister Christine celebrated their Golden Jubilee in 2010. I didn't attend. It was too painful even after all these years. Twenty-eight years within the walls, two outside. I took exclaustration (outside the cloister) in 1985 and returned in 1987, in time to celebrate my Silver Anniversary of Profession. Ever the romantic, I thought the grace of the occasion would carry me through, and I wanted to give the marriage another try. My return lasted three years, a time of being an outsider, the one who had left, a person watched closely by superiors and eyed suspiciously by novices, a worldly person. Returning to Saint Cecilia Academy after a ten-year hiatus, I related better to the girls than I ever had, tolerant of their foibles, interested in their affairs of the heart, wiser in making the teaching of the Church more tangible and less threatening to their fragile consciences.

I was a curiosity to my students as well, the nun (technically we weren't nuns, but explaining the difference—nuns are cloistered and take solemn vows; sisters work outside the cloister and take simple vows—gets tiresome) who had been "out in the world." I tried to fit in, to be the Sister Mary Anthony of old, but the rules no longer applied to my path. I wasn't religious in the way I had been taught; I was spiritual in a way I had learned on my own. I wasn't so much disillusioned as reillusioned. The divorce became final on July 22, 1990, the Feast of Saint Mary Magdalene, that fallen woman of the New Testament who became a patron of the Dominican order because she preached the resurrection to the skeptical apostles.

Our community had kept the traditional white habit and black veil through the aftermath of Vatican II. I loved it and for years was proud to be seen in it. One of the first inklings that I had of a psychological shift in my self image began in my forties, when I felt uncomfortable wearing the habit in public, especially with a large group of sisters, being stared at in the Protestant South, being called penguins. I felt myself wanting to be "singular" (a great flaw in community), wanting to be anonymous, to simply blend into the crowd. It was a shift Thomas

Merton felt once on a busy street corner in Louisville when he had briefly traded the habit for a clerical suit and collar to go to the dentist. He saw all the people in the big city going about their secular business and suddenly felt that he was one of them, not someone set apart (the literal meaning of sacred). So taking off that habit, the outward sign of my inward consecration, for the last time made me sadder than I could have imagined and relieved at the same time. Who was I without it? Stripped of the corporate image, bare of the security and belonging the habit had provided, I felt vulnerable in a way that I could not explain even to myself, although I had worn secular clothes the two years I was away. This was different, though. I would never again kiss the scapular as I entered the chapel, or feel the weight of the veil, or the rosary on my belt swaying with the rhythm of my stride. I understood why some friends who had left told me they had secretly kept their habit, buried in a drawer or hanging in the back of the closet. We had all imagined we would be buried in it, our vows rolled up in our hands, the scapular placed over our face as it had been during the profession ceremony, a sign of our death to the world.

I still sense that loss when I visit the cemetery where so many of the Sisters I knew are buried. I, the outlier, will not lie there. The first Sister Mary Anthony is there, and I always start at her grave even though she died before I joined the community. I was the second Sister Mary Anthony. There is a third now, a lovely young sister whom I met recently. There's finality in that, too. My friend and novitiate companion, Mother Ann Marie, who always prayed that I would return, has finally given away my name. I can't go home again.

That the motherhouse of Saint Cecilia was home is true in a sense that no place I lived before or since has been. One of the older sisters who taught me French in high school used to walk the grounds long into old age. We met up occasionally on our solitary walks and talked briefly. Something she said on one of those strolls stayed with me over the years, a pearl of great price pressed tightly in memory's hand and often recited like a mantra: "I am a friend to this place." Her name was Sister Mary Agnes, and I still recite her words over her grave.

Sometimes between waking and sleeping, I used to retrace my steps through every room of that cavernous building, wing by wing, room by room. I don't do it anymore because as large as it was then, the motherhouse is larger now, new wings, new rooms, containing no memories of my time there. What was a small provincial Southern community of mostly Southern women, with schools in Tennessee and a handful of missions in surrounding states, has become an internationally known branch of the Dominican order, with far-flung missions in the United States and abroad. In my day we were about 120 sisters, able to fit into the larger summer refectory and the old chapel for our annual retreat.

Everyone came home at Christmas and in the summer in those days; when the community room overflowed, we spilled outside at recreation, usually in groups of novitiate companions or sisters from our previous missions. Even as novices, we knew every person by name, even the finally professed we weren't allowed to speak to. It is hard to imagine the entire community, triple the size of ours, is ever in one place at one time now. The new chapel, so much larger and grander than the one we knew, is already too small after ten years, and nowadays there are multiple retreats. Mother Ann Marie has a full-time job just knowing them all by name, not to mention getting to know each sister on her annual visitations. I'll wake up one day to find that the Congregation has split into provinces like the Dominican Fathers, north, south, east, and west; then too, Canada, the Netherlands, Italy, Ireland, Scotland, and Australia. No third world countries yet, but that may come if the Pontificate of Francis lasts long enough and recruits keep coming to Dominican Drive in Music City, USA.

My nocturnal meanderings through the hallways and stairwells and dormitories of old were partly inspired by Thomas Merton's *The Sign of Jonas*, in particular his epilogue, "Fire Watch," when he would roam silently through the sleeping abbey from basement to belfry, keeping watch for fires and keeping vigil over his brothers, all the while musing on his place among them and in the universe:

> Lord God of this great night: do You see the woods? Do You hear the rumor of their loveliness? Do You behold their secrecy? Do You remember their solitudes? Do You see that my soul is beginning to dissolve like wax within me?[3]

There are rooms that no longer exist now, the Drying Room, the Typing Room; the Old Library and Senior Corridor; the De Profundis Hall with its naked pipes where we performed the Atrium, a symbolic hand washing before entering the Winter Refectory; the Novices Trunk Room where the "white-veils" clandestinely showed the "blackbirds" how to make the *venia*, a prostration signifying humility, made on oc-

casions slight and solemn, from entering the chapel late to ac-
cepting a penance or formal obedience. We silly postulants pri-
vately referred to it as "hitting the floor." Even if they were still
there, I would be barred from entering those and other parts of
the cloister now, for I am a "secular," one of the worldlings not
allowed in the sanctum sanctorum. I am still welcome but no
longer a member in good standing. There is freedom in that,
although not the exhilaration I felt twenty-five years ago when,
as they say, I leapt over the wall. But there is sadness too, then
and now, an abiding sense of paradise lost.

The initial fear of "losing my soul" no longer haunts me.
Soon after I left, I accompanied my friend Jean Nicholson to
the Abbey of Gethsemani in Kentucky for a private retreat and
poured out my soul to our retreat master, expressing my guilt
that having once said "for all my life," I had taken my life in my
hands and returned to the world. This monk, not my hero Father Louis but one who had known him, assured me that I had
not disappointed God but only myself, that I had done all he
expects of us, taken the next good step and followed the light
as I saw it.

Wandering Merton's abbey—at least those parts of it open
to women—and especially walking through the woods among
the knolls he loved to visit (his hermitage, the place apart from
community he had always craved), my mind returned to Father
Louis's closing words in that great prose poem that seem from
this distance a premonition:

> And now my whole being breathes the wind which blows
> through the belfry, and my hand is on the door through

which I see the heavens. The door swings out upon a vast
sea of darkness and of prayer. Will it come like this, the moment of my death, will You open a door upon the great forest and set my feet upon a ladder under the moon, and take
me out among the stars?[4]

Soon after I left, fearing that I would write an exposé of the
community, based on my recent unpleasant dealings with her
and other experiences that she felt had left me "bitter"—that
blanket term describing those who interpreted religious life dif-
ferently than their superiors and usually (how I admire those
exceptional women who stayed and fought the battle within)
chose to leave the community—the Prioress General sought out
my friend Sister Mary Bernard and asked her to intercede with
me not to write the story she feared I would tell. My friend, who
knows me better than anyone, both as a writer and as a person,
said, "I told Mother that it isn't in you to do that." And it wasn't.
And I didn't. It wasn't that I closed my eyes to injustices I had
witnessed and experienced, abuses of power in the name of obedience that crippled the consciences of the vulnerable, some
who later left and some who chose to stay and "offer it up."
Those of us with sturdy psyches recovered; some who were vic-
tims of mistreatment in the name of religion will never recover.
But I felt it was not for me to strip away the façade of piety and
expose the hypocrisy. Judgment isn't cured by more judgment,
righteous though it may be. God is the Judge. Thomas Merton
put these words in God's mouth, "Have you had sight of me,
Jonas my son? Mercy within mercy within mercy." And Pope
Francis has proclaimed this year, 2016, as a Jubilee Year of
Mercy. *Misericordia,* the heart's forgiveness. Compassion, feel-

ing with the other, co-suffering. (Hebrew, *hesed*, which contributes to *tikkun olam*, repairing the world; Arabic, *Ar-Rahman*). In the three monotheistic religions, the Merciful and the Compassionate are among the most beautiful Names of God.

I learned a lot about myself in the Novitiate, that time of introspection and self-examination and solitude. Among the prescribed rituals, meditation, chant, the daily *horarium* or schedule of prayer, manual labor, study, and recreation, I learned to walk with my hands under my scapular and keep custody of the eyes, to ring the bell when my turn came, to wait at table, to tidy the area assigned to me, to keep ordinary and profound silence at their allotted times. The Rule states that profound silence is observed "From the last signal at night until after Prime the following morning" (simply put from lights-out at 10:00 p.m. until after Morning Hours, Meditation, and Mass the next morning). As postulants, we didn't read the fine print that silence was also enjoined at all times in the cells (bedrooms) and dormitories. One day during the postulants' bath time (we did all things in unison), the seven of us were singing in our separate cubicles, talking, laughing, and throwing bars of soap over the partitions. This wasn't boarding school, but sometimes we forgot that. I was the first to emerge and found our Novice Mistress, Sister Marie William, leaning against the door, arms folded, unsmiling. I cleared my throat and whispered, "Should I tell them you're out here, Sister?" She replied, "That would be wise, my dear." So I raised my voice and announced her presence, only to be hooted down by my raucous companions. As each one came out, the racket decreased until the last culprit stood before our superior, shame-faced and profoundly silent.

By the time I got the habit, I had learned the silence rule to the point that I lost sight of common sense and even the common good, *silentium ad absurdum*. Once in the dead of night, my friend Sister Michelle, who was a chronic insomniac, especially when she was bell-ringer, shook me awake and said, "Mary Anthony, wake up, the barn is on fire!" I mumbled, "Leave me alone, it's Profound Silence, you'll get us in trouble!" Michelle, who was the boldest and least reverent of us, said, "To hell with Profound Silence, this place is burning down!" and pulled me out of bed. We ran over to Senior Corridor to alert the Prioress, Sister Mary Frances, who sounded the fire alarm and woke the house to imminent danger. Disaster was averted and we rule-breakers were heroes.

The novitiate windows on the third floor offered a view of the cemetery and west lawn, bounded by a low stone dry wall, dating from the Civil War. The "secular city" lay beyond the wall, notably North High School, and on Friday nights its floodlit football field was visible. Marida, Linda, and I had gone to high school together and hearing the band and cheering crowd increased our nostalgia for old Notre Dame throughout the fall season. North High was also our voting precinct, and the sisters formed a long line in the fall of 1960 to cast their votes for the nation's first Catholic president, John F. Kennedy. On Saturdays when the recreation period was extended, we could play certain approved records, mostly instrumental and light classical music, no rock and roll. We wore out the album, "Autumn Leaves," by Roger Williams. I suppose each of us secretly attached a name to the line, "But I miss you most of all, my darling, when autumn leaves start to fall."

We learned "Plays and Games" in the old gym, taught by Sister Virginia, a glamorous and graceful sister who was a drama major at Catholic University. She taught us things we could use later with the children we would teach, such as "Duck, Duck, Goose" and square dancing. We got penances for calling the bathroom off the gym "The Pink Powder Room." Slang was a frequent matter for penances, as when we quoted Charlie Brown's "Sigh" (*Peanuts* was big in the sixties; there was even a "Gospel According to Peanuts") or yelled "Way to go" when someone made a base hit or a home run. We played a lot of softball, pinning up our tunics so we could run faster. Another recreational activity was walking to the Jewish Cemetery in North Nashville. Along the way we passed a small pasture where I once stopped to pet the horse that came to the fence to look at us. I heard a man shout something and asked my companions, "What did he say?" as the horse snatched my veil and started shaking it. Sister Ann Marie answered, "He said that horse bites!" A novice when I entered, Sister Ann Marie Karlovic is now Prioress General. We were stationed together at Overbrook when she was principal of the Academy and again at Our Lady of Mount Carmel School in Newport News, Virginia. We were not far from the Outer Banks of North Carolina, and I have fond memories of our walks on the beach at Nag's Head. Although she is now head of the community I left, Mother Ann Marie remains my close friend, and I count on her prayers.

By the first Thanksgiving, our chronic homesickness had become acute. Apart from family and the traditions surrounding it, this holiday lost much of its charm. "The community is now your family." But the formality with which we related to one another and the institutional aspects of daily life made this concept hard to accept on an emotional level. And then, at the end of November, came our first experience of death in the convent, when our Freshman Composition teacher, Sister Cornelia, died suddenly. She was only in her fifties, a vibrant, witty woman whom I idolized. Her niece, senior novice Sister Mary Walter, Joan Seigenthaler, later went with me on my first home visit. She remains a dear friend since those days when Sister Mary Walter was the oldest novice and Sister Charlotte the youngest postulant. Mingled with my personal grief over the loss of Joan's Aunt Delia were the powerful images of ancient rituals surrounding the death of a Dominican: the bell tolling as the professed sisters donned their black mantles and gathered with lighted candles to meet the body at the front door; singing the *Salve Regina* and chanting the Office of the Dead, the all-night vigil at the open casket followed by the Requiem Mass, the procession to the grave, chanting then and for eight days afterward the *Libera me, Domine* (Deliver me, O Lord) and the *De Profundis* (Out of the depths I cry to you, O Lord). Sister Cornelia Brew was as Irish as they come and Dominican to the core. It still delights me that the simple cross marking her grave is the only one that contains the letters OP after her name. I'm not sure how that anomaly came about; the Seigenthaler name and Sister Cornelia's close friendship with Mother Joan of Arc probably played a role, but as the Irish say, "It warms the cockles of my heart" every time I visit her grave, for she was the first teacher I had who embodied the authentic spirit of the Order of Preachers, love of Truth wherever it may be found, the value of learning for its own sake, and the recognition of God-given talents in every person as a pearl of great price. Not to mention a sense of humor and unwillingness to take oneself too seriously.

Among the bits of self-knowledge I gained in the Novitiate, I also learned that I was a poet. The rhythm of the day, determined by the hours of the Divine Office, left predictable intervals of free time in small portions. My father had given me a portable typewriter for my last birthday at home, and I learned to husband my leisure moments to hover over my precious Underwood in the old Typing Room. When people ask why I don't write novels, the easy answer is that fiction is not my gift, and in my formation as a writer I didn't have time. Poems can survive interruption better than prose; at least that has been my experience. There was always a journal in my prayer stall ready to receive the odd jot, or the notebook in my pocket (nuns' pockets, such a mystery!). The fifteen minutes of *lectio divina*, spiritual reading, gave me an excuse to write not only pious words of the spiritual masters but my own words. I copied quotations in commonplace books that inspired me not only for their sentiment but also for their style. My early efforts at writing verse were terrible in the main, flowery and stilted and derivative, almost as bad as the pious platitudes that suffused my letters and cards to my parents. But I persisted and became the unofficial novitiate poet. My novice mistress encouraged my talents in the spirit of Saint Dominic who fostered the intellectual gifts of his friars. "To contemplate and to give to others the fruits of one's contemplation" was the motto of the order he founded in the thirteenth century. By the time I was in perpetual vows and teaching on the missions, my Juvenilia, works writ-

ten between 1960 and 1965, appeared in print under the title
Brief Blue Season, a slim volume of poems and verse dramas, the
latter heavily influenced by my infatuation with T. S. Eliot.
Most of this has not stood the test of time, I'm afraid, and my
few glances at it over the years cause me embarrassment. But
some of the poems are striking in their simplicity and sincerity.
I own them; they are mine. Near the end of my time at Saint
Cecilia in 1989, Maggi Vaughn, now Tennessee's poet laureate,
published the mature work of my religious life in a book auda-
ciously titled *Sister Woman*. I never thought we would get by
with the title, the Prioress General at the time being not a fan
of mine to say the least. But she allowed my friend and the community's finest scholar, Sister Mary Bernard, to be *censor libro-*
rum, and there it was, *Sister Woman* for all time, *per omnia*
secula seculorum.

Many of the poems were dense and difficult. Some of them
were sensuous, if not sensual, and later got me into trouble, although by that time I was mentally if not yet physically out of
the convent and didn't care. The influence of Gerard Manley
Hopkins and Saint John of the Cross permeates that period of
my work, and my own more mature and singular voice was
emerging out of the crucible of my turbulent forties, a period
of upheaval in my personal life, when the dichotomy of a deeper
spirituality and lesser religiosity was taking hold. I was a mess,
but my poetry was not; it was getting real, becoming pure, while
emotionally I was falling apart.

My friendships both in and out of religious life kept me together through that time. We had been taught in formation to
be general in our affections within community, all things to all

people, never exclusive. The frequent warnings about "particular friendships" were at first mystifying and later a source of humor and intrigue as we began to wonder what the phrase was a code for, what our superiors were really saying by the veiled parlance we irreverently termed "PF." How can a close relationship be otherwise than "particular?" This person in particular is my friend, not in the plural, singled out among many companions, chosen from the crowd, special in the way that John was special to Jesus. The realization gradually dawned on us that the unspoken warning referred to lesbian attachments. Even though I'm sure that among that many women there were likely to be a few lesbians, I never knew apart from hints and guesses who these deviants were. As happens when women live in a world without men, friendships, mine included, were often intense and emotionally charged. Hero worship abounded in the early years, when we fixated on and imitated older women we admired. My old friend Patsy Terrell Park, then Sister John Patrick, called them our "chinkers," referring to the *chink, chink* of the incense boat against its chain. She wanted to be "a tall skinny nun" like her chinker, Sister Mary Philip. Our peers were boon companions, partners in the daily round, kindred souls. In the rarified atmosphere of seeking perfection, the unreachable status of being "Brides of Christ," we saw and admired that striving in one another and in some few the beating heart beneath the bland exterior of uniform dress and decorous behavior. As our biological clocks inexorably ticked on, we longed for intimacy and fulfillment as women. We couldn't be wives and mothers, but by God we could give our hearts away, love one other person passionately if chastely.

> Both nuns and mothers worship images,
> But those the candles light are not as those
> That animate a mother's reveries,
> But keep a marble or a bronze repose.
> And yet they too break hearts—O Presences
> That passion, piety or affection knows,
> And that all heavenly glory symbolise—[5]

We formed strong bonds with other sisters, laypersons we taught with, priests. Even as a child, I had crushes on priests. I wanted to *be* one, for heaven's sake! That door was firmly closed in the fifties; even if future attempts to breach it should succeed, I doubt if women will be ordained in my lifetime. The road I took was the only one open; becoming a nun was second best. I have priest friends today who are treasures beyond price.

Father Jim Viall, twelve years my senior, tall, urbane, eloquent and incredibly handsome, used to give retreats to our girls at Saint Cecilia Academy. Once, after consuming too much feast day wine, I told him I worshiped the ground he walked on. He laughed and took it in stride. He was my pastor later at St. Rose of Lima in Cleveland and now, in his eighties, remains a close friend and confidante. Father Peter Heidenrich was nine years my junior, a Dominican then, too. He was my soul mate, my third brother. A mutual friend of ours in my community, Sister Philip Joseph Davis, once told him, "You are a male Sister Mary Anthony." We weren't sure if she meant it as one, but we both took it as a compliment. Father Peter's downfall at Saint Cecilia was his popularity. He was young, attractive, and wise beyond his years. On one of his visits in the early 1980s, the sisters flocked to him for confession and spiritual guidance. Many of these had been Mother Assumpta's charges when she was novice mistress, and she apparently saw this turn of events as a threat to her authority. Disregarding the injunctions in canon law against interfering with the right of religious to choose their confessors and spiritual directors, our major superior, without warning or explanation, abruptly told Peter to leave. He was devastated by this rejection and asked me what he was to do, down to the practical matter of getting to the airport. I called Mary, who as always was willing to help. She picked him up at the back gate and drove him to the airport, where he was able to catch an earlier flight and return to Chicago. Neither of us ever recovered from this cruel decision. I went to visit my family the following Christmas in 1984. It was the first time I met my future sister-in-law, Cheryl Merin. She is a psychologist who knew from our first meeting how depressed I was. She thought to herself at the time, "David didn't tell me his sister was mute." I spoke little on that visit, aside from a long conversation with Peter over the phone in which we shared our sadness at the breach of hospitality he had experienced and the harsh legalism that Mother Assumpta had injected into a religious community we both loved. Peter later left the order but not the priesthood. He always intended to write a letter to Mother Assumpta, who by this time had left our Nashville congregation and founded her own in Michigan. That letter remained unwritten when my friend died suddenly last year. Peter cannot speak from the grave, so I speak for him here. I drove to Chicago with my friend, Rebecca, in a blinding snowstorm for his funeral. I will grieve for him until the day I die, with thoughts that lie too deep for tears. So my particular friends, male and female, in and out of the convent, have sustained me from my postulant days to the present moment.

If I have a gift for friendship, and I have been told that I have, it is by the grace of having read a letter by my early hero of Dominican life, Bede Jarrett, who as provincial of the English Province in the 1930s, brought the Blackfriars back to Oxford for the first time since the Reformation. I loved Father Bede above all for his humanity and the value he placed on friendship. To a young man struggling with the inevitable tension between the vowed life and the human heart, he wrote a letter that became my personal anthem in the quest to love the Word Incarnate and the incarnational world, the "infleshness" of religion at its best and most authentic. Bede Jarrett, the "stout and elderly provincial," as he called himself in his letter to a young friend told him:

> You were in love with Our Lord but not properly with the Incarnation. You were really afraid. You thought if you once relaxed, you'd blow up. You bristled with inhibitions. They nearly killed you. They killed your humanity. You were afraid of life because you wanted to be a saint and because you knew you were an artist. The artist in you saw beauty everywhere. The would-be-saint in you said 'my, but that's frightfully dangerous.'

In trying to allay his young friend's scruples regarding a relationship with another young man in the order, Father Bede reminds him—and me at the crucial time in formation that I read his words:

> Now a cloister is not a defence but a battlefield. Your novitiate was not to protect but to train you. You are not to be

saved from meeting evil but from being overcome by evil: 'He did not say thou shalt not be tempted but thou shalt not be overcome' (Mother Julian, God bless her). . . . You must not be afraid of looking for him in the eyes of a friend. . . . You must love Y and look for God in Y. I agree that to say that your desire to bring God to him is sufficient justification for your friendship is all bunkum. It is terribly like pretending. I hate those dodges and subterfuges. You love Y because you love him, neither more nor less, because he's lovable. You won't find any other sincere reason however hard you try.

Bede Jarrett concludes this letter, so full of common sense and consolation, with a prayerful reminder that I memorized as a novice and have whispered to myself and recounted to my friends in moments of both the grief and ecstasy that friendship and love open our hearts to:

> Keep reminding yourself that God is in him and that God is in you: that you're both monstrances of God. Enjoy your friendship, pay the price of the following pain for it, and remember it in your Mass and let him be a third in it. The opening of *The Spiritual Friendship*: Here we are, thou and I, and I hope that between us Christ is a third.'[6]

In his last Thanksgiving card, Father Peter wrote, "You are someone who really knows how to be a friend." Thank you, Father Bede.

Laughter in the convent was the coin of the realm. Things were always funnier in the chapel. My first time to be versicularian as a novice, I, the youngest, was paired with the oldest novice to lead the chant with our newly practiced versicles or chants. It was a hot day in August in our small chapel packed with sisters home from the missions. There was no air conditioning in those days, and two huge fans stood on either side of the sanctuary, loudly stirring the sweltering air. As it happened, two coffins stood in the middle aisle; a pair of sisters who had died a day apart lay in state between us as we solemnly made our way to the front, bowed to each other and began to chant. Trying to avoid the caskets, we misjudged the distance between us and knocked heads. We both became unhinged and giggled uncontrollably. So did the rest of the congregation, until smothered snickers became a tidal wave of hilarity. As the laughter crescendoed, we two mortified novices tried to get control of ourselves by taking deep breaths, at which point the elder novice's belt broke and her rosary beads clattered to the floor. It was the point of no return. Only two sisters managed to continue chanting the office choir to choir, Mother Joan of Arc on her side, answered on the other by Sister Terence, a close friend of one of the deceased Sister Perpetua, whose sorrow overcame her urge to laugh. This moment of mayhem became a legend, often retold for the entertainment of those who came along later. It was so outlandish that no embellishment was needed to regale future generations. Our sense of humor saved us from ourselves and the serious business of striving to be saints.

All that convent lore was hard to part with when I left. How good and how pleasant it was when brethren dwelt together in unity. But though much was taken, much abides. And not every memory was fraught with sweet nostalgia. I was the cause of and was caused much pain as middle age set in. I was all in during my twenties and thirties, a true community person. In my forties, the dream I had constructed began to unravel. There was trouble in paradise. In the throes of first fervor, one doesn't think of the years of aridity and mediocrity ahead, when one doubts not only her own vocation but the idea of vocation itself, of a calling to transcend the limitations of self and the venality of institutions, however exalted their purpose. Perhaps Merton's journey to Bangkok was a way to leave the monastery without the finality of leaving it. His sudden death and return to be buried in the ground he loved was a mercy, and a little joke that only he and his hidden God, *Deus absconditus*, could appreciate, a chuckle at the Abbot's expense. I was envious. There would be no finish in a blaze of glory for me. My first departure was awkward and full of anxiety. I just needed to get away for a while and asked to make a private retreat in some neutral place. That being denied, my only recourse was to take the official leave canon law provided.

Books had always sustained me in the past. Both as a religious and as a teacher of literature, I had cherished the Fathers of the Church and the spiritual classics, including Bernanos's *The Diary of a Country Priest*, the poetry of Charles Péguy, the English metaphysical poets John Donne and George Herbert, and the works of T. S. Eliot following his conversion, especially "Ash Wednesday," which I always read to my English classes at the beginning of Lent, his verse drama, *Murder in the Cathedral*, and above all, Eliot's great poem of the soul's quest for God, *Four Quartets*. In the last of these, "Little Gidding," I found the woman who then and now fanned the fading spark of hope in me that "all shall be well and all manner of things shall be well"—Dame Julian of Norwich and her *Book of Shewings: Rev-*

elations of Divine Love. Through her I discovered the other English mystics. In the fog I moved in, bereft of certainty and spiritual consolation, I clutched *The Cloud of Unknowing* with both hands.

In the crisis year 1985, after a quarter century as a Nashville Dominican, I was long past à Kempis's *The Imitation of Christ* and Saint Thérèse's *Story of a Soul.* The writings that sustained me now were Hopkins's "Terrible Sonnets":

> Wert thou my enemy, O thou my friend,
> How wouldst thou worse, I wonder, than thou dost
> Defeat, thwart me? Oh, the sots and thralls of lust
> Do in spare hours more thrive than I that spend,
>
> Sir, life upon thy cause. . . .
>
>   . . . . birds build—but not I build; no, but strain,
> Time's eunuch, and not breed one work that wakes.
> Mine, O thou lord of life, send my roots rain.[7]

Aridity is the term the spiritual writers use, but I didn't then and don't now presume to place myself in the mystical dark night of the soul during that period. I didn't feel that special; just burned out and dry and wondering if these bones could live again. So into that vacuum, as they say, a book . . . It seemed true in my case that when the student is ready the teacher will appear. Somehow, I believe by grace, I found *The Kingdom Within: The Inner Meaning of Jesus's Sayings,* by Episcopal priest and Jungian psychologist, John Sanford. In his chapter, "The Inner Adversary," Sanford quotes Matthew 5:48, "You must therefore be perfect just as your heavenly Father is perfect." The very touchstone of religious life, the raison d'être of the evangelical counsels of poverty, chastity, and obedience is embedded in this passage. I knew it all by heart, and I knew that I had failed in the pursuit. Then came the interpretation I had never heard, and it changed my perspective on everything I thought I knew about Christ and the gospel and myself. My life would never be the same once I had read this passage. The sword of the Spirit cut my heart in two, and there was no going back to my former self and religion as I knew it. These are the words I read that seared my soul:

> There is probably no saying of Jesus subjected to more abuse than this one. The very way in which it is translated into our English Bibles does violence to its profound and paradoxical meaning, for "you must be perfect" brings to our minds the image of abiding by a perfectionist moral code that allows us no shadow, no taint of impurity or imperfection—in short, that does not allow us any possibility for reconciliation with the inner enemy.

I had recently completed a master's degree in Sacred Scripture, requiring a reading knowledge of New Testament Greek. But the impact of one passage failed to make a dent. The Greek word rendered "perfect" means literally "brought to an end state." Sanford makes it so clear:

> It is not a matter of achieving some impossible saintlike condition, but of being fulfilled as the person we were created to be. We are to be complete or whole, our lives and personalities brought to the conclusion that God has intended, not perfect in the narrow and one-sided meaning of the word. It is this completeness, this paradoxical wholeness, that is the goal of the kingdom of God, and it can be estab-

lished only in persons whose very faults and failures have contributed to the development within them of their highest potential and greatest capacity for love.[8]

These are the people Jesus describes as "cunning as serpents and yet as harmless as doves" (Matt 10:16). Finally, I had found what I was thirsting for: the Christ of the Paradox, the Parable Teller (*para-bole*: to throw together unlike things) was telling me that life, even the life of perfection, is full of ambiguity; that the truths of Catholicism truly are *mysterium fidei*, mysteries of faith; that here we see as though in a glass, darkly, and no one, including those deemed our superiors, sees the whole picture, least of all what is in our heart's core; that good and evil are as long as this world lasts locked in each other's grip (*mors et vita duello conflixere mirando*) "in combat stupendous" (Sequence for Easter Sunday). Sanford sums up what Jesus means by being perfect in terse but powerful words: "Such wholeness will be extremely paradoxical".[9] His chapter concludes with the story of the sinful woman forgiven much because she loved much, in John Sanford's interpretation "more than a story of forgiveness":

> What is meant is that we are to live intensely, even if this means we can no longer avoid blame. The Pharisee, by always playing it safe, sought to remain blameless before God, but as a result he was not emotionally involved with life and people as was the woman who was a sinner. She found greater love than the Pharisee, and she was made whole, for in spite of her sins she had lived.[10]

It was a quiet revolution I was involved in, a secret upheaval, but I could no longer look at scripture, or my superiors, or myself in the same way. Where this new knowledge would lead me

I did not know, but I knew what was required of me: to simply take the next good step, to follow my best lights, believing in him who said, "I am the Way and the Truth and the Life," and trusting as Thomas Merton had that the desire to please him does in fact please him and that he would never leave me to face my perils alone.

During that time fraught with inner turmoil and anxiety, I often thought of my sweet Jesuit Gerard Hopkins, exiled in Dublin, unknown to the world as a poet until the next century, bewildered and bewildering, a stranger in a strange land. I didn't have to write my own terrible sonnets. He had written them for me.

> Cheer whom though? The hero whose heaven-handling flung
> me, fóot tród
> Me? or me that fought him? O which one? is it each one?
> That night, that year
> Of now done darkness I wretch lay wrestling with (my God!)
> my God.[11]

There was no shadow, no taint of impurity in the ritual of my first profession of vows on March 10, 1962. My parents came from Florida and brought my cousin Carol Jean with her first child, baby Rhonda. A new life for her, a new life for me.

Amo Christum

I love Christ into whose chamber I shall enter; whose mother was a virgin, whose father knew not woman, whose voice speaks to me in gentle tones. Whom when I touch I am pure, whom when I have accepted I am a virgin. He has pledged his troth with his ring, and he has adorned me with his precious jewels.

At nineteen I knew no other reality; I was espoused to Jesus Christ; what more did I need to know? I was Eve in the Garden, before the serpent appeared. I could only see the dove and believe in the innocence that youth and grace and the generosity of self-giving contained. The year before I had worn a wedding dress and bridal veil and carried lilies to the altar, then knelt to hear a new name and receive a new garb:

> "Sister Mary Anthony, what do you desire?"
> "The mercy of God and yours and to be received to the holy habit of Saint Dominic."

By 1965, the Second Vatican Council had rejected the ancient monastic tradition of religious women being *Sponsae Christi*, "Brides of Christ." The Church was moving into the modern world. The religious habit was to be modernized, simplified to a dress suited to active service in the world. By the 1970s many communities had discarded it altogether and with it monastic practices such as cloister, common prayer, silence, penance, and corporate apostolates such as teaching and nursing. The great exodus from convents and monasteries was underway. The teachers who had played a role in my vocation in high school were gone, as were many of my peers. A friend asked why I wasn't leaving too, since Saint Cecilia was doomed to disappear. I remember my reply, stated with resignation if not conviction: "I guess I'll go down with the ship."

Teaching was my escape, indeed my salvation, in those turbulent years. The decade I spent at Saint Cecilia Academy was busy, challenging, and fulfilling. I poured myself into my work with those high school girls, and I was good at it. I was strict and demanding in class. My courses in English, history, and religion were rigorous and my reputation as a hard teacher was legendary. But outside the classroom I was approachable, at least by seniors—underclassmen kept their distance—and immersed in their extra-curricular activities. I sponsored the newspaper, the yearbook, the Senior Class, headed the English Department, attended the students' plays and athletic events, counseled the doubtful and consoled the sorrowful. My partner in all this frenetic activity and friend to this day was Sister Mary Evelyn. The girls called us the twins because they couldn't tell us apart from the back. We had boundless energy, zeal for souls, a sense of humor, and we didn't know how to say no to the projects that superiors and principals heaped upon us—even fundraising which we detested. These days, we often look at each other and ask how did we do all that and still keep the demanding schedule at the priory with its own set of duties: sacristan, laundress, bursar, procurator, bell-ringer, reader at table, cook, hebdomadarian (weekly leader for the Divine Office), and all the minutiae of daily life in a large house? Our answer, usually in unison, "We were young and didn't know any better." Then we laugh and shake our aging heads to think of our heyday, the '70s. Now we're in *our* 70s. That was then, this is now. I have taught in other secondary schools since then: Webb, Baylor, briefly my alma mater, Notre Dame. But Saint Cecilia Academy got the best of me. I've never given elsewhere what I gave there, or had it to give.

Two other factors contributed to the happiness and apostolic success of those years at Overbrook. We lived on campus and could walk to the three schools we served, SCA, Aquinas

College, and Overbrook School. We were available to our students and their families; they, in turn, saw how we lived and could join us for Mass or Vespers. Although the White House, the jewel in the crown on those 92 acres, was an impressive building rivaling any in West Nashville or nearby Belle Meade, our living quarters were anything but lavish. Senior faculty occupied a few rooms upstairs, but we younger sisters slept in Quonset huts attached to the back, literally a barracks built to be temporary but housing us way past its prime. A few of us also lived in the attic, a hideaway we loved and vied for until the fire department finally declared it unsafe for human habitation. More than any practical advantage to being stationed at Overbrook, we were blessed to have Sister Anastasia as prioress. She was stately, dignified, and a talented musician who taught music for years and ran the community's largest mission and only priory outside the motherhouse with the same patience and light touch her music pupils enjoyed. Among them were Rebecca Horton for whom Sister Anastasia was mentor and abiding inspiration for the best one could be in religious life. Rebecca was organist for the Cathedral of the Incarnation for years and is a brilliant pianist. Sister Anastasia's niece, Sister Mary Herman Horn followed her aunt to Saint Cecilia and shares both her dedication to duty and musical ability. I recently learned that my publisher, Eric Killinger, took piano from Sister Anastasia and remembers her with great fondness and nostalgia for those childhood days in Nashville.

Our number varied from twelve (minimum for a priory) and twenty in those days, and a motley crew we were. Sister Henry Suso Fletcher, first president of Aquinas College, was an innovative and farsighted administrator, highly respected in academic and corporate circles in Tennessee, who gained the support of other entrepreneurs for her bold programs that put our little college on the map. At home Sister Henry was famous for her lavish cherries jubilee and bananas foster desserts; her Christmas eggnog recipe was legendary and yes, potent. Sister Mary Robert (Mona Manning) was so talented that she could have been a concert pianist and one of the most flamboyant characters I ever knew. Her jam sessions in the Recreation Hall at the motherhouse were a happening. Young and old would gather round as she played from memory any song we requested, always ending with the Notre Dame Victory March. Mary Robert's teeming imagination devised our own Peanuts gallery at Overbrook. She of course was Schroeder, Sister Mary Bernard was Lucy, Sister Terence was Linus, Sister Mary Peter was Frieda, Sister Mary Albert was Peppermint Patty, Sister Mary Leonard was Snoopy, Sister Mary George was Miss Othmar the teacher, Sister Ignatius was Charlie Brown, and I was his little sister, Sally Brown. Only Sister Mary Robert could have gotten by with this and Sister Anastasia in her tolerant (and secretly amused) spirit, let it be. Something intangible was lost when the priory at Overbrook was closed in the 1980s and the faculty lived at the motherhouse, commuting to our campus schools. No longer could students waiting for late rides home linger in the front hall listening to us chant the evening Office, or knock on our door when they needed a wise word for a weighty matter or just an after-hours chat; no longer could I offer the rare privilege of holding Honors English for a small group of seniors in the parlor. Being across town from our classrooms and our students might have become more practical, but there were immeasurable losses, undetectable to long-range planners and corporate goals. The White House holds the administrative offices for the Dominican Campus now, a more efficient use of space and resources. I hope, though, that one day Dominicans will live on that land again, perhaps in a new priory or even a novitiate house. I was, after all, a friend to that place. I taught again at Saint Cecilia, from 1987 to 1990, between my first departure and my final one. It was my swan song. I no longer had the strength or stamina to be that legendary teacher. Neither did I desire to be. I had been to hell and back by then. I knew a thing or two about the world and my place in it. I was wiser, more tolerant, and more human. The second time around, I had Charlotte Barr in tow. I had another life. I gave them that.

But back to the life that was, the life I vowed. Final profession took place on June 13, 1965. I was not yet twenty-three and still believed in the possibility that I could be all that I had hoped to be when I entered religious life. It was an auspicious day not only for the ceremony that marked it but also for the fact that it was the Feast of Corpus Christi and my feast day, Saint Anthony's Day. I can still recite from memory the words I uttered that day:

> To the honor of Almighty God and under the protection of the Blessed Virgin Mary and of our Holy Father, St. Dominic, I, Sister Mary Anthony Barr, make to God in your hands, Reverend Sister Marie William Macgregor, Prioress General, the simple vows of poverty, chastity, and obedience for all my life, according to the Rule of St. Augustine and

the Constitutions of the Dominican Sisters of this Congregation of St. Cecilia.

That was the summit. The irrevocable step had been taken. No higher high ever surpassed the feeling, dare I say the ecstasy, I experienced that day. No more ceremonies of commitment awaited me. From then on it was back to "the more austere but happier way of living," as St. Augustine expressed it in his rule. Or as the common vernacular would put it, it was all downhill from there. The daily routine, the rounds of duty lay before me, punctuated by the festivals of the liturgical year, which broke the monotony and even at times evoked the splendor of that day in June.

Christmas and Easter, made more intensely splendid by the austerities of Advent and Lent, were a wondrous time in the convent, preceded by exhaustive preparation and exhausting work, culminating in Midnight Mass and the Easter Vigil when we were giddy with fatigue and anticipation. I especially loved Advent, that "brief blue season," its quiet joy and emptiness teeming with inchoate life. Being the youngest postulant meant holding the door for the entire line of sisters walking in order of precedence. But it also meant, that first Christmas, carrying the infant Jesus to his bed of straw. Had I come all this way for birth or death? For birth, surely.

Far from the hectic commercialism of our busy sidewalks, I came closest to the Advent of those convent years in Austria and Prague with Father Peter in 2011, when we prowled the Salzburger Christkindlmarkt and prayed in the Stille Nacht Kapelle of Oberndorf and visited the crèche of Domkirche St.

Stephen in Vienna and walked the cobbled streets of Telc in Moravia and roamed the streets of Praha, Prague, the golden city of spires, crossing and re-crossing Charles Bridge, hanging out in Wenceslas Square, and celebrating Mass at the Shrine of the Infant of Prague. The Infant who has a vast wardrobe of cloaks wore purple for Advent. It was our last trip together. Father Peter was closer to heaven than we dreamed, but that was our heaven, the antechamber at least. We'll always have Prague.

At some point, I copied on a blank page of my Rule and Constitutions a list of Permanent Values or Intrinsic Requirements of the Dominican order:

I. VOWS

II. ASCETICISM

III. SACRED LITURGY

IV. STUDY OF TRUTH

V. COMMON LIFE

I want to explore a bit my relationship with the fourth, the Study of Truth. I was no scholar in high school, although even then teachers and classmates recognized that I had a way with words. The sister who taught me senior English wrote in the comment section of my report card, "Does only the minimum."

And she was right. I had other fish to fry, as we say in the South. I hated chemistry, although I loved my teacher, Sister Mary James (she later left, married a priest, bought a farm, raised horses, found her inner artist, and remains a close friend). So I dropped Chemistry after one semester and took typing from another teacher I admired, Sister Terence, who later became my principal at St. Cecilia Academy before she, too, left. I never memorized the keyboard and still type with two fingers. My claim to fame my senior year was being editor of the yearbook.

I learned to study in the convent; it was simply what Dominicans did. One just didn't bring home any grade below a "B." And I took to it with a relish that surprised me. I was hungry for knowledge, not just Thomistic theology, though that was de rigueur, but truth wherever I could find it. Saint Cecilia is a teaching community, and it gave me, along with my religious formation, an excellent education. I loved teaching literature, especially Shakespeare and poetry. Later in teaching both biblical theology and the Bible as literature, I felt that my learning had come full circle. In the years since my formal education ended, my love for the words of great literature and the Word of God has enriched me beyond measure as a person and as a poet. The Word made flesh is not only the bedrock of Christianity but is as well the wellspring of human art. Saint Dominic's Order of Preachers was the conduit for me of Christian humanism, and I have not ceased to be grateful for what it gave me. My blood still runs black and white.

So did Father Peter's. His reasons for leaving the order were as complex and compelling as mine, though our experience of Dominicanism was different. But his training helped to make him the great preacher and apostle that he was, just as my identity was irrevocably entwined with Sister Mary Anthony's. We made a journey to Italy with several of his parishioners in the fall of 2007. After a flight from Zurich to Milan, we took a bus through Genoa to Ligouri and the Italian Riviera, touring the magnificent Cinque Terra from Rapallo on the Adriatic. Then it was on to Pisa and the city we both loved so much, Florence. We took day trips to Siena, San Gimignano, and the vineyards of Tuscany, and from Tuscany to Umbria and Assisi the home of our beloved Saint Francis. Finally, our pilgrimage wended past Perugia through the Apennines and ended in Rome. There were many stellar experiences on that trip, including visits to the tomb of the Dominican Saint Catherine of Siena and mass at the tomb of Saint Francis surrounded by Giotto's marvelous paintings of the early Friars Minor, and High Mass on a Sunday at the Basilica of Santa Maria Maggiore. But for Peter and me, nothing compared to our secret visit apart from our companions to San Marco in Florence, home of the early followers of Saint Dominic. It was October 16, a day we both agreed we would never forget and always cherish, as we visited one by one the cells of the medieval friars, each one containing a fresco by Fra Angelico. By then, neither of us was a member of the order hallowed in that place. We were no longer officially Dominicans. But we each knew in our heart of hearts that we would always be members of Saint Dominic's family.

I took with me to his funeral my old watch fob with the Dominican crest and motto: *Laudare, Benedicere, Praedicare*: To Praise, to Bless, to Preach. As I stood at the foot of his casket, I dropped this old token of our shared past into the folds of his vestments. *Vale, Frater.*

The tipping point of my decision to take exclaustration in 1985 was the celebration of Saint Cecilia Congregation's 125th Anniversary of the founding in 1860. Mother Assumpta had removed me from Aquinas College after the first semester and brought me back to the motherhouse in a raging snowstorm because she knew my intention and wanted me where she could watch me closely. Her official reason for this was to put me on the 125th Committee, which proved to be my Waterloo. Previously, I had told my brother, David, that I was planning a leave of absence. His brotherly advice was practical: "Get a driver's license." So I used my committee work as an excuse to take this necessary step toward independence.

In the previous General Chapter, my position as a delegate had given me a forum for my cause, poverty. Our section of North Nashville was a depressed area through the mid-eighties; Germantown was only beginning to be gentrified, and Metro Center was in the very early stage of development. We were the White Ladies in the Big House on the Hill surrounded by poor black neighbors in their ramshackle rental houses. Vatican II's "preferential option for the poor," so prominent now in the era of Pope Francis, was not a priority in our community. We took few schools in the inner city, and didn't stay long when we did. There was no program of outreach to the surrounding community, although the Sisters who ran the kitchen dispensed many a sandwich at the back door. Rebecca later told me that the scales fell from her eyes one day when she encountered an elderly lady who asked if Sister could take her to the grocery store. She made the mistake of asking permission and was told no. I reminded her of something we both knew in hindsight, "Forgiveness is easier to get than permission."

So there we were, planning an extravagant anniversary party, and there I was, helping to plan it. Around the same time, the Sisters of Mercy celebrated their centenary with a dinner of soup and bread, the benefactors' contributions going to their various ministries. We didn't get that memo. Mother Assumpta was a familiar figure in Rome in those days, and she would bring Rome to Nashville. Two cardinals were flown in at the community's expense, the Prefect of the Sacred Congregation for the Clergy and the Pro-Theologian of the Pontifical House, along with the Cardinal Archbishop Emeritus of Saint Louis. Two archbishops, eleven bishops, the Master General of the Order of Preachers in Rome, the provincials of the Southern and Eastern Provinces of the Dominican Fathers, along with numerous priests, seminarians, and deacons were in attendance. Most of these, especially the higher ranking clergy, were housed in the only building comparable to ours in size, recently constructed behind the motherhouse, the splendid Maxwell House Hotel. Being scandalized is a word overused and misused in religious circles, but I was well and truly scandalized. Besides, I was exhausted by the work I had done to prepare for this event and feeling terribly guilty for my part in it.

And so, in lieu of the private retreat I requested and was denied, I took the separation allowed by the Church. Overbrook Priory, scene of some of my happiest years, was vacant for the summer, so I left from there, precluding the possibility of other sisters, particularly the novices, seeing me in lay clothes. After we had signed the necessary papers and Mother departed, taking my habit with her, I took a cab to my friend Mary's house in Belle Meade. Her husband, Rob, fixed me dinner—his specialty, "Brookfield Grill"—showed me to the guest room, and the next day drove me to the airport. I flew to Edinburgh, where Mary and her children, Gwynn and Bob, were waiting for me. It was a storybook ending to a traumatic period of my life, being with my best friend and her precious children in the border country of Scotland, my father's ancestral home. I was grateful and relieved beyond measure, but I was also an emotional wreck, now moody and depressed, now giddy and hysterical with laughter. I was the third kid, and Mary was the grown-up. Gwynn and Bob quickly adapted to seeing me out of the habit and continued to call me "Sma" as they do to this day. We lived in a rental cottage in the Borders; gorged ourselves on clotted cream and Cadbury bars; watched Boris Becker win Wimbledon; took long hikes; drove to the Lake District, crowded to our disappointment with tourists and caravans; tramped through ruin after ruin—the children never got enough of them; visited Sir Walter Scott's cavernous pseudo-medieval castle and estate; and had high tea on the lawn of a family Mary knew on the Firth of Forth, where Gwynn picked raspberries, a lovely scene I later wrote a poem about. This sensitive, deeply religious young woman is about to embark on studies for the Episcopal priesthood. And little Bob, who loved his Legos and had a laughing fit with me over Black Forest Pie at the Copper Kettle in Kelso, is now the loving father of his own little girl. Yes, Mary, Gwynn, and Bob: Scotland Forever! My healing began there.

By the time I left Scotland, I was ready for the next phase, getting a job and getting out of town. Our chaplain at Overbrook, my friend and spiritual advisor, Father Bill Nolan, connected me with Marie Cirillo, a former sister herself and a no-nonsense organizer from Brooklyn, now the head of Appalachian Ministry for the Diocese of Nashville. She had organized a land trust in Campbell County, the state's poorest, bordering on Kentucky and Virginia, a region in the heart of coal country, where most of the men had black lung disease, the women were the breadwinners when there was work to be had, and the children did their homework by the glow of candles or kerosene lamps. The stereotypical broken down cars in their yards were there not because their owners were lazy and slovenly but because the bad roads blew out their tires, and they couldn't afford gas to run them. My Aunt Sarah and Uncle Ray drove me from their home in Morristown by snaky mountain roads to Marie's house in Rose's Creek, a "holler" in the Clearfork Valley. Aunt Sarah did not want to leave me in that "Godforsaken place" and cried as they drove away.

Marie loaned me a summer cabin up the hill and paid me $50 a week when there was work. She and I were living the reality of poverty we had once professed in theory. I was on food stamps and wearing secondhand clothes from thrift stores. I was happy. I admired Marie and was proud to do my little part to assist her ministry. We drove her pickup truck to a hunger conference in Minneapolis, co-sponsored by TVA and In Our Own Way, a woman's organization for social outreach. My signal professional achievement in the six months I stayed at Rose's Creek was a project interviewing mountain women from the bordering mining towns of Clairfield, Tennessee, St. Charles, Virginia, and Barwick, Kentucky—coal country—and recording their stories. I saw myself immortalizing these proud and resourceful people as James Agee, my fellow Knoxvillian, had the sharecroppers in his seminal work, *Let Us Now Praise Famous Men*, during the Depression. I called my manuscript of these collected interviews "Hungry Moon," and my brother, David, wrote a theme song for it. His lyrics and those women's faces, captured in their wizened beauty and rugged dignity by the brilliant photographer, Warren Brunner, of Berea, Kentucky, haunt me still:

O hungry moon, shining through the hollows
Of the mountains of my home:
They've got us on our knees.
Digging black wealth from the ground,
Killing all the streams and cutting all the trees.
O hungry moon, shining through the hollows
Of the mountains of my home.

My dream is to publish this document one day and let these strong women, some from the grave now, have their say before a wider audience than was available in 1985. On a personal level, my shining achievement was making friends with Daisy Pierce and helping to pay off what she owed on her land. Daisy was my age, 43, but looked twenty years older. Without the benefit of cosmetics and proper diet, mountain women wrinkled early and lost their teeth. For most, false teeth and even eyeglasses were beyond reach.

The winter that year was brutal. I was living in an uninsulated summer cabin, sleeping with two adopted mountain dogs for our mutual comfort and warmth. When morning came, there was frost on the carpet, and I could see the breath from my cold lungs. It was no surprise that I came down with double pneumonia by Christmas. Providentially, a former Dominican, Louise Born Bush, who was Supervisor for Special Education in Shreveport, Louisiana, called me to extend holiday greetings and express her concern for my present plight. I can hear her now, "Charlotte, you are going to die in those mountains. Come down here, and I will get you a teaching job." But how to get there? It was Mary Crichton to the rescue again. I couldn't rent a car without a credit card, so she used hers. Marie took me to Knoxville to pick up the rental, and I drove to Nashville, said goodbye to Mary and my mother, and headed out to Louisiana with my dogs, Rose and Sister. When I got to Shreveport, Louise had to hang all my clothes outside because they reeked of kerosene. She got me that job teaching middle school for the Caddo Parish School System. I had always said I would never teach in the public schools. Never say never. I taught at Youree Drive Middle School for the next year and a half and moonlighted selling fine jewelry at Zales in one of the area malls. I lived with the Bushes for six weeks until I could afford to rent an apartment and after that became a permanent guest at their Sunday dinners. Louise's husband, Walter, who had been pastor of the parish church where I grew up in Chattanooga, helped me start my first checking account and loaned me a car for the duration. Louise and Walter, their daughters, Imelda and Marie, as well as their one-eyed Boston terrier, Lady, became my family; displaced person that I was, I certainly needed one. Walter died several years ago, but Louise, who is now married to Steve Rider, remains one of my closest friends. I can never repay her for harboring me during my leave of absence and helping me to adjust to life in the world beyond St. Cecilia. As she prepared those famous Sunday dinners, Louise and I used to swap stories of our frequent convent dreams. Mine usually involved being late for prayers and unable to find all the pieces of my habit or my office book. She had a recurring dream of going back to Saint Cecilia after her daughters were born and not knowing what to do with the children. In one dream, she kept looking for a closet to hide them in. Louise tried to talk me out of going back, but I had the romantic dream of celebrating my Silver Jubilee of Profession. My mother came down to help me clear out my apartment and pack. We used the money from selling my furniture for a visit to New Orleans, and my savings to finance Mom's dream of going to Ireland, the ancestral home of her Dean family. Then I was ready—or thought I was—to return to Saint Cecilia in August 1987. Four of us were left to renew our vows. Our fifth companion, Sister Mary Lawrence Levering had switched from the Roman to the Eastern Rite and became Sister Theodora in Nazareth, Israel. She was fluent in French, a brilliant musician and artist, and has graced her monastery in the Holy Land as she had ours with her gifts of nature and grace.

Meanwhile, I was enjoying a short-lived second honeymoon at Saint Cecilia, full of joy and hope that I could be as I had once been, a devoted member of the community I loved. My family had mixed feelings about my comings and goings during this unsettled period. My father, a devout convert, was proud of his Dominican daughter. He died in 1974, and I've often wondered if I would have had the courage to leave had Dad been living. My mother was aging and needed me. I knew that one day I would have to leave in order to care for her, fulfilling the role of only daughter. My unconventional brother, Nelson, had settled in Tucson, far from the madding crowd and drug scene of his New York past. His daughter, Charlotte Faitha Anna, my godchild, was named for all the women in his life: Nelson's wife Charlotte; Aunt Charlotte; our mother, Margaret Faitha; and Charlotte's mother, Ann. Whew! My brother,

David, an atheist since college, had always thought my renunciation of career and marriage a waste and worried about the responsibility of supporting me financially if the community no longer did. He got me an American Express card the first time I was on my own and paid the balance the first year. Through the years, David and Cheryl have come to my rescue more than once, most recently paying my property taxes. When I finally cut ties with Saint Cecilia and moved back to Chattanooga with our mother, David was very supportive of our decision to live together and delighted when I joined the faculty of the Baylor School, his alma mater as well as that of our father and all the Barr uncles.

I returned to Saint Cecilia on the Feast of the Transfiguration, August 6, 1987, in the twenty-fifth year of my religious profession. I was home and, for a time, content to be that person I had vowed to be in 1962. But I gradually learned that I was no longer that person, try as I might, and three years later I finally accepted the inevitable. Soon after my return, Louise brought the girls to visit me at the motherhouse and told me later that Imelda and Marie said as they drove away, "Mom, you can't leave her there, she isn't happy. Let's go back and get her." The wisdom of children, who see beneath our exterior to the person we don't know we are. They are mothers themselves now and professional women like Louise. Walter would be so proud of them.

One of my first discoveries was that I had lost active and passive voice by taking exclaustration, meaning that I could neither vote nor be voted for in an election. So, without my participation, a new Prioress General came into office in 1988. She was not only my novitiate companion, Ann Born; she was also Louise's younger sister. So for a time, all was well with me in the realm of higher authority. But the watershed was 1989 when *Sister Woman*, a collection of over twenty years of my mature religious poetry, was published. Although she had given permission for its publication, literature was not her forte, and Mother had not actually read most of these poems. Things came to a head when my friend and former colleague at Aquinas, Victor Judge, wanted to publish an interview regarding my work in the *Peabody Reflector*. The timing for this project couldn't have been worse, since one of our sisters had recently sent a less than prudent diatribe about abortion to the diocesan newspaper without permission. As a result, the ultimatum had come down from on high that no sister could publish anything for public consumption without prior perusal and approval by the Prioress General. So Victor asked his questions, which I answered honestly but with trepidation. Being the splendid professor and interpreter of literature that he is, Mr. Judge quoted extensively from my poems in the article. He reluctantly gave me a copy for censorship purposes, and I dutifully left it on Mother's desk. A couple of days later, I went back to get the manuscript, Victor's deadline looming, only to be told that it could not be published. I asked the question one didn't ask superiors: Why? What followed is seared in my brain, every word of hers, every word of mine. Suffice it to say here that the focus of her objection was my poem, "A Complaint to Her Lord in Her Loneliness," written sixteen years before and previously published in the *Sewanee Review*. This poem, one of my best, is replete with the spiritual eroticism one finds in the Old Testament's Song of Solomon, in the poetry of San Juan de la Cruz, in Bernini's *Saint Teresa in Ecstasy*. A critique of this poem by Anthony Kerrigan, Senior Guest Scholar at the University of Notre Dame, appeared on the back cover of *Sister Woman*, plainly visible for all to see:

> Sister Mary Anthony Barr uniquely represents in the English speaking world the divinity of Eros in a totally un-Puritan Mare Nostrum (mediterranean) Catholicism. She sings the spirituality of the sensual, and the sensuality of the spiritual, there is no split in her psyche between thought and feeling, between spiritual thought and sensual feeling. Her verse is devotional in its aspiration toward the condition of godliness. She is illuminated by grace in the transcendence of all sensory—and "past sense"—loveliness. And she courts God as sweetly as Teresa de Avila, though she is even more incandescently visual.

To simplify her objections, Mother's verdict was, "It is not who we are." And in that moment a bell sounded in my head; it was an aha moment, an epiphany, the point at which I knew in the core of my being that I would have to leave this community, that I did not belong here anymore. It was true, what she was saying, they were not who I was; I was not who they were and never could be again. I left her office, knowing that I had just experienced a moment of truth, a Damascus event that would change my life forever. I was both extremely sad and enormously elated. I could go now and not look back. I am, from the perspective of twenty-five years, grateful to Mother Christine. She was the catalyst, indeed the instrument of grace, for the necessary and painful decision I had lacked the courage to make until that moment of truth in her office.

I decided to tell no one I was going this time and quietly got my ducks in a row, as Mary put it when she said, "You're not leaving here this time around until you have a job." My publisher and friend, Maggi Vaughn (that indomitable woman who asked at our first meeting, "Honey, don't you have any play clothes?") arranged a secret meeting with Jon Frere, headmaster of Webb School in Bell Buckle, who hired me to teach English and be poet-in-residence. The only sister privy to my plans was my friend, Sister Rose Marie, Secretary General of the congregation and our only canon lawyer, who got me the proper forms. Since Saint Cecilia is a pontifical rather than a diocesan institute, my request for a dispensation had to be written to the Pope himself, according to a prescribed formula:

PETITION FOR INDULT OF DEPARTURE
TO HIS HOLINESS JOHN PAUL II

(To be written in applicant's own hand on plain stationery)

His Holiness Pope John Paul II
Apostolic Palace
Citta del Vaticano
Italy 00120

Most Holy Father:
I sincerely ask you to grant my petition to be dispensed as soon as possible from the perpetual vows, which I took as a member of the Congregation of Dominican Sisters of Saint Cecilia of Nashville, Tennessee, on 13 June 1965 (date of final vows).
The reason why I ask for this release from my vows is the fact that I am not able to persevere in fulfilling them. The

reasons why I am unable to do so are:
(Briefly but concretely detail the actual reasons motivating
the request. Indicate what means—spiritual, psychological,
or medical have been used in order to resolve existing problems.)

My reasons follow:
I believe that it is necessary to have support in community
in order to live the vowed life fully, as a response to grace,
which respects the dignity of the person called by God. It is
not sufficient that such support be intentional; it must be
actual. I can no longer bear the burden of the vows because
I no longer experience their blessings in the concrete. The
common life and religious authority, as means to an end, are
meant to assist, not impede, my following of Christ. I fear
that remaining a member of the Congregation of Saint Cecilia will compromise my integrity, impede my spiritual
growth, and put my relationship with Christ at risk. I come
to this decision with regret, after years of prayer, discern-
ment, and spiritual direction. My attempts to resolve existing problems include two years of exclaustration from June
1985 to August 1987. In the three years since I returned to
my religious house, I have seen with deeper clarity that this
is the only course I can take.

With sentiments of reverence and devotion, I remain

Obediently yours in Christ,

Sister Mary Anthony Barr, OP
(Religious name)
Margaret Mary Charlotte Barr
(Secular name)

The response, not from the Pope himself, but from the Prefect for the Sacred Congregation of Religious Institutes, was

written 22 days later—speedy by Vatican standards—and I signed my dispensation, officially titled ACCEPTANCE OF IN-DULT OF DEPARTURE AND WAIVER OF ALL CLAIMS, on July 22, 1990, in the library of Villa Maria Manor, my mother's residence, witnessed by my former major superior, Mother Christine Born, OP.

Sister Rose Marie kept my plans to herself until the day I left. She drove me to my mother's apartment, returning to find a notice that her presence was required at an emergency meeting of the General Council. She never said at what personal cost she had helped me, but knowing her sense of privacy and profound integrity, I know she was willing to pay it. She had written on the envelope of documents and instructions I requested, "Sister Mary Anthony, don't do it." But she never stood in my way and trusted that I was following God's will as I saw it. I can never repay her for being an integral part of that will and for remaining my friend. I could not bear to tell Sister Mary Bernard, a dear friend to us both, so Sister Rose Marie told her I had gone and delivered the note I had written. I had taken them all—and myself—by surprise. As my friend, Sister John Marie (later Gerry Schaefer Till), once said while scrubbing floors on her hands and knees during Holy Week and looking out the open front door of her mission house: "Hello, World." I turned 48 that August. And I was newly born.

It was a long time before I could go back to the mother-house. But I return now at least once a year to see old friends, trade stories and relive memories with those I shall always count among the sweet years, and, of course, to visit my mentors, teachers, and friends of old in the cemetery. They see it all clearly now, how we strove and how we failed, what was essential and what was peripheral in what was asked of us; how silly some of the rules were, and yet how weighty the endeavor to live the spirit of the law was. They understand my ambivalence, being glad I went and glad I left. I am learning in my seventies to live with the paradox "Of what was believed in as the most reliable/ And therefore the fittest for renunciation" (T. S. Eliot). I stand at their graves and accept that I cannot be buried among them but that I am still a friend to that ground.

Charlotte Barr

Ash Wednesday/Holy Week 2016

Written in Light

A Photographic Memoir

"Bring flowers of the fairest . . ." Our Lady of Perpetual Help Church, Chattanooga, 1943. I could barely walk, and David wasn't in school yet; but Nelson and our lifelong friends, Betty Carroll and Cherie Wells, wore white for the May Procession.

Holy Ghost Church, Knoxville, 1948. I was a first-grader chosen to carry the flowers. The sun blinded both flower-bearers on that May day. The boy in the bow tie on the left was my brother, Nelson. The priest on the right, Father Joseph Follman, brought my father into the Catholic Church shortly before I was born.

"Bride of Christ," Saint Cecilia Convent, March 5, 1961, the day I received the Dominican habit and a new name, Sister Mary Anthony.

Reception Day with my parents, Margaret and Nelson Barr; my brother, David; and my Flower Girl, Susan "Bunny" Terrell. She carried her sister's flowers the following year when my childhood friend, Patsy Terrell, became Sister John Patrick. She left before final vows, married, and named her son John Patrick.

(Photo: Joe Horton, Joe Horton Studio, Nashville)

First (Temporary) Profession Day, March 10, 1962, when I vowed Poverty, Chastity, and Obedience for three years. I was nineteen years old.

The three Chattanoogans: Sister Luke Hollerbach, Sister Mary Angela Highfield, and Sister Mary Anthony Barr. My two novitiate companions celebrated their Golden Jubilee of Profession in 2012.

(Photo: Joe Horton, Joe Horton Studio, Nashville)

Mother Joan of Arc Mayo, OP. She instructed my mother in the Catholic faith in the 1930s and was Prioress General when I entered in 1960 and received my first vows.

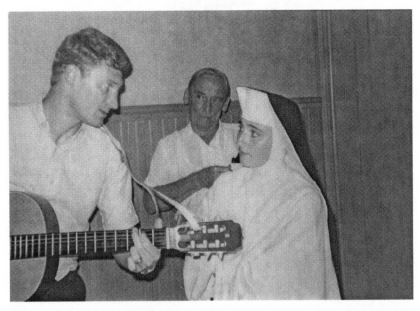

David serenading Dad and me in the Guest Dining Room, 1962. After that visit, my father wrote: "It was almost like having a real home life again with you and David around."

First year teacher, Saint Patrick's School, McEwen, Tennessee, 1963. It was a small country school between the railroad tracks and the cemetery. I was the youngest of three sisters on this mission. The other two were in their 50s and 70s. I taught first and second grade in the same classroom. It took the Community two years to realize that I was not cut out to be a primary teacher. I knew it the first day.

School pictures over the years. Thank goodness the flattop veil went out after Vatican II!

Signing my final (perpetual) vows, June 13, 1965, witnessed by Mother Marie William MacGregor, who had been my novice mistress.

(Photo: Joe Horton, Joe Horton Studio, Nashville)

Nelson as Dominican novice, Brother Reginald, with Dad at Saint Joseph's Priory, Somerset, Ohio, August 15, 1961, the Feast of the Assumption and his 25th birthday.

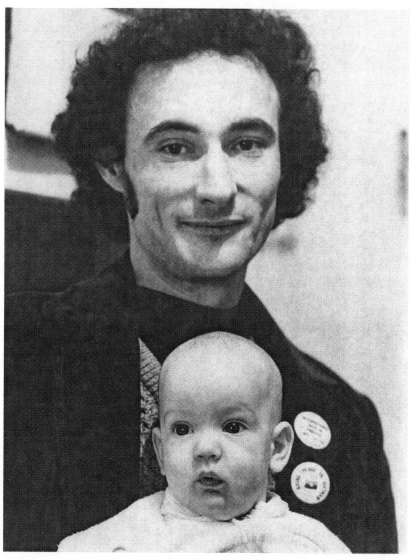

Nelson the activist with his son, Joshua, New York City, 1965. Joshua's Jewish mother left Greenwich Village with him two years later and severed all ties with the Barr family. My parents never saw their first grandchild.

Meeting my nephew, Christopher, at my parents' home in Hollywood Beach, Florida, Christmas Day, 1967.

Chris with his daughter, Taylor Marie—David's first grandchild—at our family gathering in 1995 at "Cloud High," the summer home of David's wife, Cheryl, and the Merin family in the Blue Ridge Mountains near Highlands, North Carolina.

Wedding Guest: Her father, John Martin, walking his daughter, Sister Mary Pius, and me down the aisle at her brother Johnny's wedding in Saint Mary's Church, Clarksville, June 1966. Before she left Saint Cecilia and all the years since, Elinor "Tootsie" Martin and I have remained friends.

(Photo: Dancey Studio, Clarksville, Tennessee)

Greeting my former student at Saint Cecilia Academy, Nan Piot Andrews, on her wedding day.

Sister Mary Walter Seigenthaler (Joan Miller) was Senior Novice and I the youngest Postulant when I entered Saint Cecilia. She was my companion on my first home visit in 1965. Dad thought of Joan as a second daughter, and our mothers became friends. In the years since we both left the convent, we have never lost touch.

My mentor, hero, and friend, Father James A. Viall.

Retreat Days for the girls at SCA in the 1970s

With Father Jim at Niagara Falls, 1978.

I taught eighth grade for two years at Father Viall's parish school, Saint Rose of Lima in Cleveland, Ohio. My mother came for a visit and accompanied Sister Mary Evelyn, our intrepid pastor, and me on the bus trip to Washington, DC, a rite of passage for graduating students. On the way, Father had his ear glued to his transistor radio, when he suddenly announced, "Habemus Papam!" It was October 16, 1978, and Pope John Paul II had just been elected.

SCA's Class of '73 Reunion in 2003. Besides Rebecca, the other Dominican from that class was Sister Mary Christopher (Vickie Weiland). Becky set the camera on time lapse and then jumped in the picture, back row, second from right.

Sister Mary Evelyn and I joined the party after recreating a classroom scene from thirty years in the past.

Always the animal lover. Saint Cecelia Academy, 1977.

Meeting my first and only niece, Nelson and Charlotte's daughter, Charlotte Faitha, named for both her mother and me, in Tucson, Arizona, June 1980.

Faitha visited Aunt Sister and the "Moms," as she called us, at Overbrook and the motherhouse for Christmas 1962.

Fast-forward: Faitha's daughter, Selkie Frances, in 2013 with the Aunt Sister doll I gave her mother when she was a toddler. One of my senior classes commissioned this strange little nun and presented her to me on Class Night. Our art teacher—my then colleague and now good friend, Jane McElroy—secretly sketched me at faculty meetings to create her.

Aside from needing her habit washed periodically, Sma has aged little in forty years. She celebrated Christmas with us when I visited Faitha, David, Jack Daithi, and Selkie in 2014.

Sister John Marie (Gerry Schaefer Till), one of my earliest "chinkers" in the 1950s.

Louise Born Rider (Sister Valerie), Gerry, and I toasting the good old days and the even better present on their visit to Chattanooga in the 1990s.

My dear friend, Mary Whitson, and I when we taught at Aquinas College together in the early 1980s. Our friendship began when we chaperoned a group of students on a trip to Europe. The tour bus almost left us behind in Dublin because we were determined to find Gerard Manley Hopkins's grave at Glasnevin Cemetery. We found it, too.

After many years and many miles, Mary and I met a baby albino camel in Palmyra, Syria, in 2008. The recent destruction of that marvel of the ancient world makes our memory of being there all the more precious.

'Friends when I needed them: Joseph Raya, Archbishop of Akka, Haifa, Nazareth, and all of Galilee. I first knew this saintly man as Father Joe, pastor of Saint George's Melkite Rite Church in Birmingham, Alabama, when I taught at Saint Rose, our private school there from 1966 to 1968. It was thanks to Father Raya that my first collection of poetry, Brief Blue Season, *appeared in print. From Israel, he retired to Madonna House in Combermere, Ontario, where my former student and close friend, Marie Therese Fajardo, is a member.*

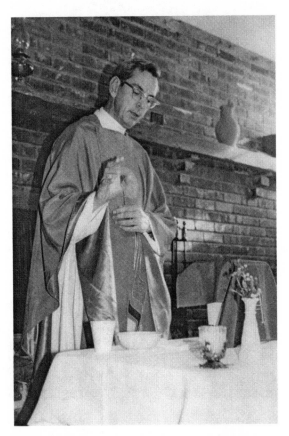

Father Victor Brown, OP. This warm and wise Dominican from New Orleans was chaplain and professor at Aquinas when I was there. He became my confessor and spiritual adviser leading up to and during my period of exclaustration. Father Brown told me to take the full three years allowed by canon law. I returned after two years. If I had followed his advice . . . one of the what-ifs in my life.

Father William Nolan. A priest and a psychologist, Father Nolan helped many of us through vocation crises while he was chaplain at Overbrook and a teacher at the college. He and Father Brown had both been novices at Trappist monasteries in their youth. Victor realized that the Cistercian cloister was not for him when he sat on a bench one day and a cat jumped into his lap. Since he liked cats, he started petting it when a monk observed this and said it was against the rules. He later said, "I knew I didn't belong in a place where I wasn't allowed to pet a cat." Bill Nolan's epiphany was more traumatic. Barely out of high school, he was performing the required manual labor of digging a ditch one day with some fellow novices. He looked up when a monk appeared to give him a message from the abbot that his mother had just died. Young Billy was not allowed to attend her funeral.

Jean Nicholson. I met Jean when she used to come to Sunday vespers at our mother-house. When I left, Jean helped me pick up the pieces of my life. A former Sister of Mercy, she understood both the beauty of religious life and the painful journey from that life that some of us must walk. Jean was a high school language teacher and is a gifted artist. The boxing nun doll I gave her appealed to her Irish sense of humor. She keeps close ties with the Sisters of Mercy and is my connection with the order that taught me at Holy Ghost and until her death with Sister Annunciata, RSM, once the head of Saint Mary's Hospital in Knoxville, who delivered me when my mother went into labor after the doctor assured her that there was plenty of time and went off to Mass that Sunday morning in August 1942.

Father Peter Heidenrich, OP. My brother in Christ and friend of friends.

Diaspora Babies. Susan Marshall Vance (Sister Jane Anne) with Peter and Timmy, Christmas 1987.

Anne Rozek Cook (Sister Anne Joseph) with Joey, Easter 1995.

Becky and I joined up with the older Dominican Diaspora generation on Saint Patrick's Day 1995 at Fairfield Glade in East Tennessee near the Great Smokey Mountains. Merri Jo Kern (Sister Virginia), Marilyn McKinness (Sister Marilyn), and Ann Alsobrook Maxwell (Sister Mary James) regaled us with their convent stories, and we drank MacGregor Scotch for auld lang syne.

With Ann and her beloved horses at the farm she and husband Alex Maxwell, a former priest, owned in Greenback, Tennessee. Ann taught me at Notre Dame High School in Chattanooga, and Alex was later principal there. Since this was their hometown as well as mine, they were also graduates of NDHS. Soon after they married, Ann and Alex attended their class reunion, and Alex famously stood up and said, "I'm the one who rode off into the sunset with Sister Mary James."

Back in the habit again. With Mom and David on the motherhouse grounds the day I returned to Saint Cecilia, August 6, 1987, the Feast of the Transfiguration.

Teaching the novices during the interim period between 1987 and 1990.

(Photo: Nancy Warneke, *The Tennessean*)

Promotional photo for the publication of Sister Woman, *1989.*

(Photo: G. W. Austin)

My mother, Margaret, and my publisher, Margaret Britton Vaughn at my reading and signing, hosted by Jean Drennen Dortch, owner of Saint Mary's Bookstore in Nashville, after the publication of Sister Woman *in 1989.*

With Sister Mary Rebecca in our "floruit" during the 1970s.

Rebecca and me after my last commencement at Saint Cecilia Academy in May 1990. Becky was a freshman in my world history class the first year I taught there, 1968–1969. When she was a senior, I taught her anthropology and English IV, 1972–1973. Entering the convent right out of high school as I had, Sister Mary Rebecca also took a leave of absence following her mother's sudden death to care for her father, who had been diagnosed with cancer. Exclaustration was not an easy choice for her, either. I helped arrange a meeting with a Dominican priest visiting our community from Italy. We will never forget his words, "Sister Mary Rebecca, the fourth commandment to honor thy father and thy mother came before the Evangelical Counsels of poverty, chastity, and obedience. Now go home and take care of your father." After Joe Horton's death in June 1991, Becky returned to community for a time. We both tried that, but for both of us the long and winding road did not lead back to where we started.

The road led me to Bell Buckle, Tennessee, a tiny railroad town near Murfreesboro, where one could find lots of antiques, a few struggling artists, and the Webb School. Becky was in the audience for a reading by the "The Bell Buckle Poets" in 1992.

Maggi and I set up our booth at the Southern Festival of Books in Nashville.

The author of The Bell Buckle Years, *at home on the Webb campus.*
(Photo: Dawn Hankins, *Shelbyville Times-Gazette*)

A rocking chair in the country with my beloved Paddington. I had imprinted as a baby on my father's Scottish Terrier, Minnie Hootnanny. After canine deprivation for thirty years, I had to have a Scottie. Pooh Barr later joined Paddington, and Paddy II, Lulu Bascottie, and Fergus Finbar followed them.

(Photo: Dawn Hankins)

Former and present Dominicans at the open house following the dedication of Saint Cecilia's new chapel and infirmary wing in 2006: Sister Mary Evelyn Potts, Annie Rozek Cook, Mother Rose Marie Masserano, Sister Mary Angela Highfield, and Charlotte Barr.

Civil War-era back porch and laundry (now the development office) in the back of the motherhouse. Stories have been shared by generations of sisters from their rocking chairs on that porch.

(Photo: Rebecca Horton, Joe Horton Studio)

Stained glass window of Saint Cecilia, Roman martyr and patroness of music, chosen by the founders as patroness of the original Saint Cecilia Academy and motherhouse in 1860. Artists came from Bavaria to create these exquisite windows when the Chapel was constructed in the late nineteenth century.

(Photo: Rebecca Horton, Joe Horton Studio)

Window depicting Saint Dominic receiving the Rosary from the Blessed Virgin Mary. This was the chapel we loved, prayed in, and eventually outgrew. It is now the chapter room and space for community meetings.

(Photo: Rebecca Horton, Joe Horton Studio)

The Nashville skyline in 2006 with the new chapel constructed during Mother Rose Marie's term as Prioress General in the foreground. I had a comparable view of the city from my window in the postulants dormitory in 1960. There was one lone skyscraper then, the Life and Casualty Tower. Nashville and I came of age together.

(Photo: Rebecca Horton, Joe Horton Studio)

Sacred Heart statue and main entrance of Saint Cecilia Motherhouse and Novitiate, 2006. This is one view that remains unchanged, except that Jesus got his fingers back in the renovation.

(Photo: Rebecca Horton, Joe Horton Studio)

Epilogue

THIS STORY IS NOT strictly chronological. I like to think that it merges Chronos, Secular Time, with Kairos, Sacred Time. Neither is this memoir complete. The whole story is impossible to tell. What I have told is the truth but not the whole truth. It is simply my truth, and not all of that, because as Eliot said, "Human kind cannot bear very much reality." This is not Saint Cecilia Convent's story but only my story as I lived it there and as I remember it. Memory is slippery and selective, but I have tried to be faithful to that part of my past, which is of course always present.

> What we call the beginning is often the end
> And to make an end is to make a beginning.

The end is where we start from. . . .
Every phrase and every sentence is an end and a beginning,
Every poem is an epitaph.

—T. S. Eliot, "Little Gidding"

I made the first attempt to record Sister Mary Anthony's story five years after I left Saint Cecilia. It was too soon. The wounds were too raw, and I lacked the perspective to tell it without rancor. I was "wild with all regret." So I put it aside. I found that first manuscript recently but resisted the temptation to read it until I had finished this one. In these twenty years since I began to record the experience, I have changed, and the community has changed, I think both of us for the better. I wanted to remember the good times, and there were many. My happy years in community far outnumbered the years of sadness and regret. It took further years of absence and distance to realize that.

We shall not cease from exploration
And the end of all our exploring
Will be to arrive where we started
And know the place for the first time

—T. S. Eliot, "Little Gidding"

In coming to terms with my past life, I also needed the insights of others who shared it. I needed my Sisters of the Dominican Diaspora, a small group of us who have gathered for the past twelve years, dogs in tow, to spend a week in the mountains together. Each of us has told the others her story, filling in the missing pieces we could only retrieve collectively. We have laughed and cried and made ourselves whole in the process.

From a safe distance we could conjure the "August 16th Massacre," for example, the term given it by my brilliant and witty friend Sister Jane Ann, now Susan Marshall Vance, who had "seen the elephant," as she so aptly called it, while serving as one of the youngest prioresses of the motherhouse, fell apart during one of our summers at Providence, and left soon after. That was the day we prepared to depart for our various missions after receiving our assignments on August 15, the Feast of the Assumption. Ironically, this ominous meeting fell on my birthday and usually ruined it. Not that we celebrated birthdays in the convent, only our name days, the feasts of saints whose names we received with the habit. So this was the day that Prioresses General corralled us before we scattered, to give us our walking papers, read the riot act. They exhorted us to practice religious decorum and observe our vow of obedience in matters grave and trivial.

We could laugh now over beer and barbecue about the reminder to always wear our little sleeves, those superfluous appendages held on with rubber bands under the copious sleeves of our tunics. To take them off, except when washing dishes or engaging in other tasks that hampered freedom of movement, was a fault worthy of reprimand, a sign of disregard for the Rule, an indication of "worldliness," along with crossing our legs at the knee (at the ankle being permitted), swinging our arms when walking, or letting our hair grow out, a sure sign someone was planning to leave. A younger sister who was on the cusp of "returning to the world" once told me, "The last thing I plan to do before I go are shave my legs."

As we sat by the Ellijay River and gazed at our precious portion of the Blue Ridge Mountains, Becky and Pat and Annie and Cathy and I knew that we had come shining through and come safe home.

> He that shall live this day, and see old age,
> Will yearly on the vigil feast his neighbours, . . .
> Then will he strip his sleeve, and show his scars.
> And say, "These wounds I had on Crispin's day."
>
> —Shakespeare, *Henry V*, 4.3.44–45, 47–48

Yes, we few, we happy few, we band of sisters, we were survivors.

Afterword

[Borrowed from *The Bell Buckle Years*, 1992]

Prologue

THE POEMS IN THIS collection are products of up-heaval and dislocation, which they, in some perhaps indefinable way, record. I came to the country from the convent, after

> Years of living among the breakage
> Of what was believed in as the most reliable—
> And therefore the fittest for renunciation.

These lines from Eliot's great prayer-poem, *Four Quartets*, accompanied me, along with the baggage of three decades in a religious community. In the throes of a painful leave-taking, I settled into my uncertain niche within a boarding school community and my place in a tiny village traditionally receptive to artists and craftsmen. People have been kind and this transitional time has been good.

At first I thought that both Sister Mary Anthony and her Muse had stayed behind in Nashville. I began to fear that I might never be able to pray or to write poems again. But in time I came to understand that the Sister and the Woman were the same person, and that vows to God go deeper than any document. Our gifts are not revoked; in the soul's night they wait, among the unseen angels, to be summoned from the shadows and attend us. I learned to pray again, and since "waking in the country" I have begun to write again.

"So here I am," to borrow from Eliot once more,

> Trying to learn to use words, and every attempt
> Is a wholly new start, and a different kind of failure
> Because one has only learnt to get the better of words
> For the thing one no longer has to say, or the way in which
> One is no longer disposed to say it. And so each venture
> Is a new beginning, a raid on the inarticulate. . . .
>
> Here and there does not matter
> We must be still and still moving
> Into another intensity.[12]

The Convent Poems

Polished Floors

Unbidden,
The convent loomed up
From my just waxed floor.
And thirty years of life
Were in the scent of
Mineral spirits and
Polished hardwood floors.
Three years gone, those
Times of cleaning before
A major feast, those
Festal days spread with
Chant and merriment,
But here again, just now,
And from now on,
As ingrained as
The pattern in
The bole.

Of Virgins

Purity abides not long
In those who gauge it,
Measuring virtue's weight
Against their own, but casts
Her eye upon the hindmost
Parts of Christendom, the
Prodigals; she too subsists
On famine's husks, the bare
Habiliment of hope.
The worst is not to sleep
Alone, but is to make of
Solitude a haven for the
Unencumbered self; the
Virgin who's not merely
Chaste, but clean of heart,
Knows this: her hunger is
Antecedent to the feast,
Her vacancy invites the
Playfulness of God.

I. Black and White

No dress or attitude admitted gray,
It was albescent day, nigrescent night,
It was a perfect world of black and white;
To one stupendous choice we said our yea,
And after that we gave our wills away,
In contemptus mundi, straining toward the light,
We labored bell to bell, and put to flight
All terrors of the night and foes of day.
Dead to the world, the world was dead to us,
The rainbow's promise came without the sign;
To earthly joy as much as earthly lust
Our guarded eyes and shrouded hearts were blind;
Creation's loveliness did see but dust,
The pale bread godlier than the purple wine.

From *The Text Beneath*

Monastic Dreams

My manumission is complete but for my dreams,
Which draw me back to corridors of silence, rows
Of veiled companions, the high, thin chant, meek
And folded hands, footfalls light in heavy clothes,
The comfort of constriction.
My waking world is wide, the broad way gleams
Wherein the heart's unhomed and, homeless, grows.
I rise to risk; athrill and trembling both, I seek
Commerce with the world, its joys, its woes,
The rub and spark of friction.
But often in the night phantasmagoric streams
Asperse me, as my shadow in procession goes
To burnished altars of the past; pale voices speak,
And soul, past reason's strength to interpose,
Implores their benediction.

Saint Anthony's Day

For SMB

We beg you . . . that the soul may safely flee to you on that
last day of affliction and fire, when the silver rope will be broken.
— St. Anthony of Padua

Ecce quam bonum et quam jucúndum habitare fratres in unum.
— Psalm 132

June thirteenth, my erstwhile feast comes round again,
And the anniversary day of my perpetual vows.
I was twenty-three; in the certitude that youth allows,
I said, "for all my life," and sure I meant it then.
St. Anthony doesn't reproach me, stays my friend,
And some companions keep my memory.
Today I think of them and celebrate what has been,
How good and pleasant still that story.

Blessing the Cells

In my dream I am blessing the cells as once I did
In another life: Saying, "Ave Maria" and signing
The cross on their curtains with the blessing of
Water in the profound silence of convent rest.
I send my sisters to sleep with these words, this
Shake of the wrist, this wish for their fretless
Sleep until dawn.
In the morning of this other life, I would rise
To ring the bell, calling them back to the
Waking life we all shared: to duty and day
And the daily round of communal prayer.
It was what it was: delight and despair and
Fondness and fear of not being all we had
Promised to be.
I am not what I promised to be in my
Floruit but believe I may come to the
Feast and be let in because of my
Friend, Whose love led me there
By a devious way, Who knows
My desire despite many turns to be
Blest and be staid.

From *Looking Up*

At the Golden Jubilee

For her three friends, these novitiate companions from another
time, joy, *gaudium*, that gladness akin to wisdom: for they are
the wise virgins, ready now as then for the Bridegroom when
He comes, to enter the joy of their Lord.
For her, *seledreorig*, sadness for the lack of a hall; for despite
their hospitality, the signs that all say, come and share our joy,
after the recessional and when the banquet ends, she knows the
silence after, when the cloister door is closed.
For they have stayed, have stood these fifty years, while she has
gone so many other places, the Hall forsaken in her peregrina-
tions; she has lived in many places and calls the last one in her
childhood city home.
For her the comfort is to know even this Motherhouse
Is but a temporal abode, however storied and secure.
There is no lasting city here, and whether they wait
Or wander, wayfarers are they still and all.

Fifty Years On

Then I said, "for all my life," and sure I meant it then,
Being twenty-two and in love; but time and trouble
Intervened and I am here fifty years on, and that day
seems but a dream.
So high my hopes then and sweet the night air that
I breathed, high above the city from my dormitory
Window, when total consecration was the rule and
all was possible.
Women are such dreamers, designed for giving life.
I was such a one, who gave up childbirth for the
Higher good, possessed by an unseen lover and his
insubstantial arms.
The world is insubstantial too and even more the
Promises it makes, the greetings where no kindness
Is, this I learned and this I know is true; so leaving
it was no loss.
And finding it again was not a gain, but just the
Knowledge that I was as I always was: a woman
Made for love and longing for that God of love,
then and now.

Notes

1. John Hill, "The Venom of Destiny: Reflections on the Jung/Joyce Encounter," *Spring 79: Irish Culture and Depth Psychology* (Spring 2008), 107.

2. Keats's letter to George and Georgina Keats was written over the course of three months—14 February to 3 May 1819. This portion, concerning the world as the vale of soul-making, was written 21 April 1819. See John Keats, *The Letters of John Keats, 1814–1821* (Cambridge, MA: Harvard University Press, 1958), 100–104.

3. Thomas Merton, *The Sign of Jonas* (New York: Harcourt/Harvest Books, 1981), 360.

4. Ibid.

5. William Butler Yeats, "Among School Children," *The Poems* (New York: Macmillan Publishing Company, 1989), 217.

6. Kenneth Wykeham-George, OP, and Gervase Matthew, OP, *Bede Jarrett of the Order of Preachers* (London, England: Blackfriars Publications, 1952).

7. Gerard Manley Hopkins, "Thou art indeed just, Lord, if I contend," *The Poems of Gerard Manley Hopkins*, 4th ed. (Oxford, England: Oxford University Press, 1970), 107.

8. John A. Sanford, *The Kingdom Within: The Inner Meaning of Jesus's Sayings* (San Francisco, CA: HarperOne, 1987), 95.

9. Ibid., 97.

10. Ibid.

11. Hopkins, "Carrion Comfort," *op. cit.*, 99.

12. T. S. Eliot, "East Coker," *Collected Poems, 1909–1962* (New York: Harcourt, Brace & World, 1970), 188–189.

About the Author

CHARLOTTE BARR WAS BORN August 16, 1942, in Knoxville, Tennessee. Soon after, her family moved to Chattanooga, where her father was employed by the Tennessee Valley Authority. As a small child, Charlotte spent several winters with her mother and brothers in Anna Maria, a barrier island off Florida's gulf coast. During high school, she lived for a year in Cairo, Egypt. She graduated from Notre Dame High School in Chattanooga in 1960.

From 1960 to 1990, Charlotte belonged to a religious order in Nashville, the Dominican Sisters of Saint Cecilia, where she was known in religion as Sister Mary Anthony, OP. She earned her bachelor of arts in English at George Peabody College for Teachers, now Peabody at Vanderbilt. Charlotte holds an MA in English from the University of Memphis and an MA in biblical studies from Providence, a liberal arts college run by the Dominican Fathers of the Eastern Province in Providence, Rhode Island.

Charlotte was a teacher for over forty years, most notably at St. Cecilia Academy and Aquinas College on Nashville's Dominican Campus at Overbrook. After leaving St. Cecilia, Charlotte taught for two years and was poet-in-residence at the Webb School in Bell Buckle, Tennessee. From 1992 to 2007, when she retired from teaching, Charlotte taught English, Creative Writing, and Western Religions at the Baylor School in Chattanooga, where she held the position of poet-in-residence.

During her novitiate year, Charlotte began seriously to write poetry. Her early convent poems appeared in the collection, *Brief Blue Season* in 1966. Over the years, Charlotte's work has been published in several periodicals and journals, including *The Sewanee Review*, *The Cumberland Review*, *The Distillery*, and *The Spire*, a publication of the Vanderbilt Divinity School. Poems by Ms. Barr were recently anthologized in *St. Peter's B-List: Contemporary Poems Inspired by the Saints* (Ave Maria Press, 2014) and *Adanna: Women and Spirituality* (*Adanna Literary Journal*, Fall 2015). Two volumes of poetry, *Sister Woman* (1989), and *The Bell Buckle Years* (1992), were published by Tennessee's poet laureate, Maggi Vaughn, at Iris Press and Bell Buckle Press, respectively. Her most recent collections of poetry, *The Text Beneath* (2010) and *Looking Up* (2015), bear the imprint of Parsons Porch Books.

CPSIA information can be obtained at www.ICGtesting.com
Printed in the USA
LVOW11s1545190616

493251LV00001B/223/P